A. Haddock.

Rock The Boat!
(Ark, Ark)

Music by Sheila Wilson
Edited by Alison Hedger

*Dedicated with love to Margaret, the kindest friend I could wish for.
Thank you; may you have all the happiness you deserve.*

To be sung as a sequence of songs, with narration and choir,
(see the Pupil's Word Booklet for the narration).
Alternatively the story can be acted out as it unfolds.

Duration of songs with narration approximately 20 minutes

For use in schools and churches
and will be enjoyed by children of all ages,
especially at Key Stages 2 and 3

SONGS

Opening Song:
1. (Noah Jazz)
In the beginning

	1. Desperate Measures	All
	2. Noah, Noah	All + some two-part singing
	3. A Load Of Baloney!	All
2x2	4a. ~~Miles And Miles And Miles~~	All (could use groups for some verses)
	5. Rock The Boat!	Noah solo
	4b. A Bit Of A Do!	All + 'thigh-slapping' interlude
Reprise	5. Live In Peace	All

Final song:
Noah Jazz.

The Pupil's Word Booklet is available separately Order No. GA11048.
A matching tape cassette is also available, Order No. GA11049,
Side A with vocals included and side B with vocals omitted for rehearsals and performances.

© Copyright 1997 Golden Apple Productions
A division of Chester Music Limited
8/9 Frith Street, London W1V 5TZ

Order No. GA11047

ISBN 0-7119-6689-3

1
DESPERATE MEASURES

All

If an introduction is required, please play bars 1–8

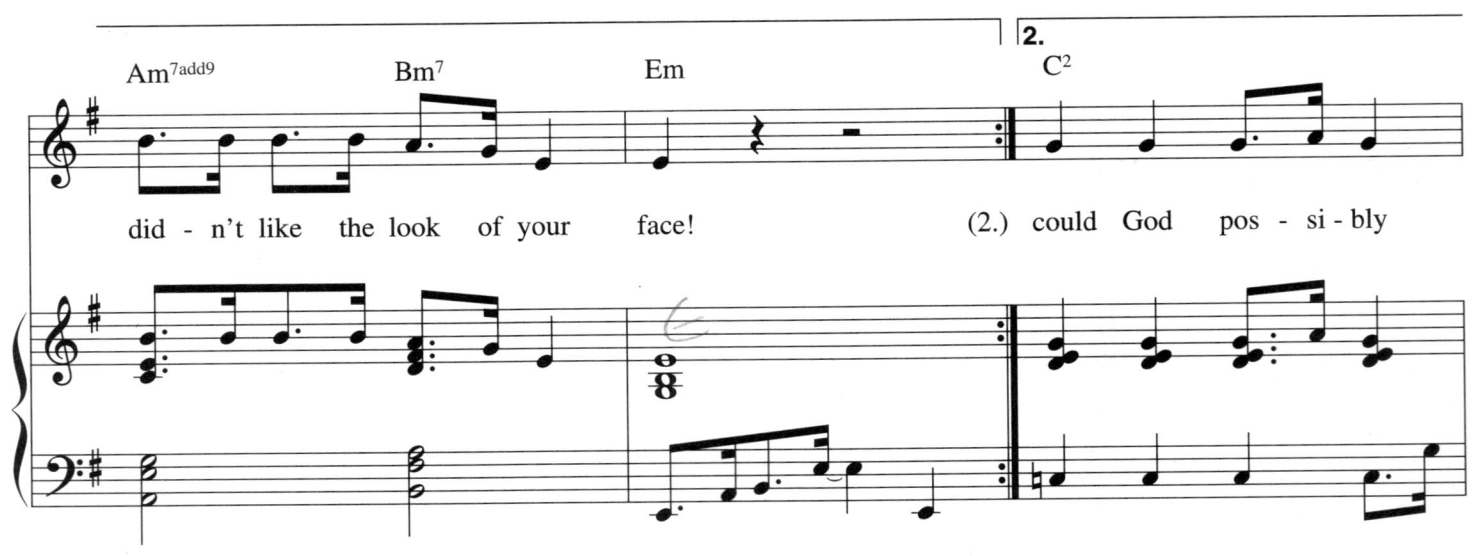
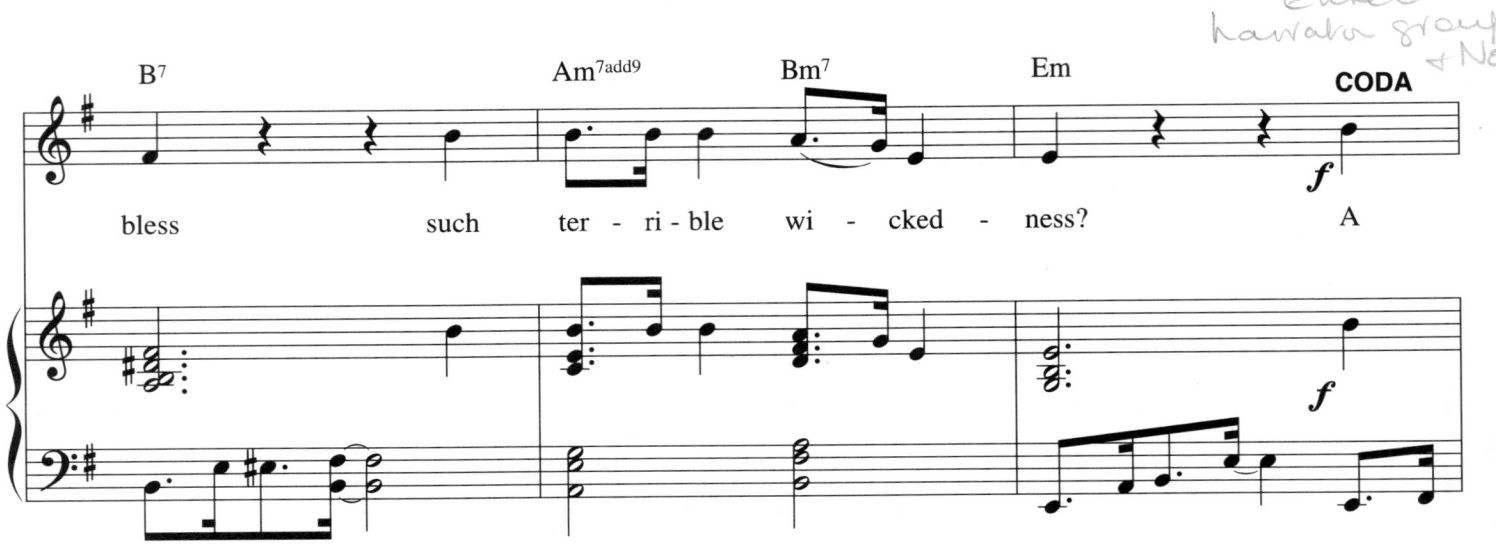
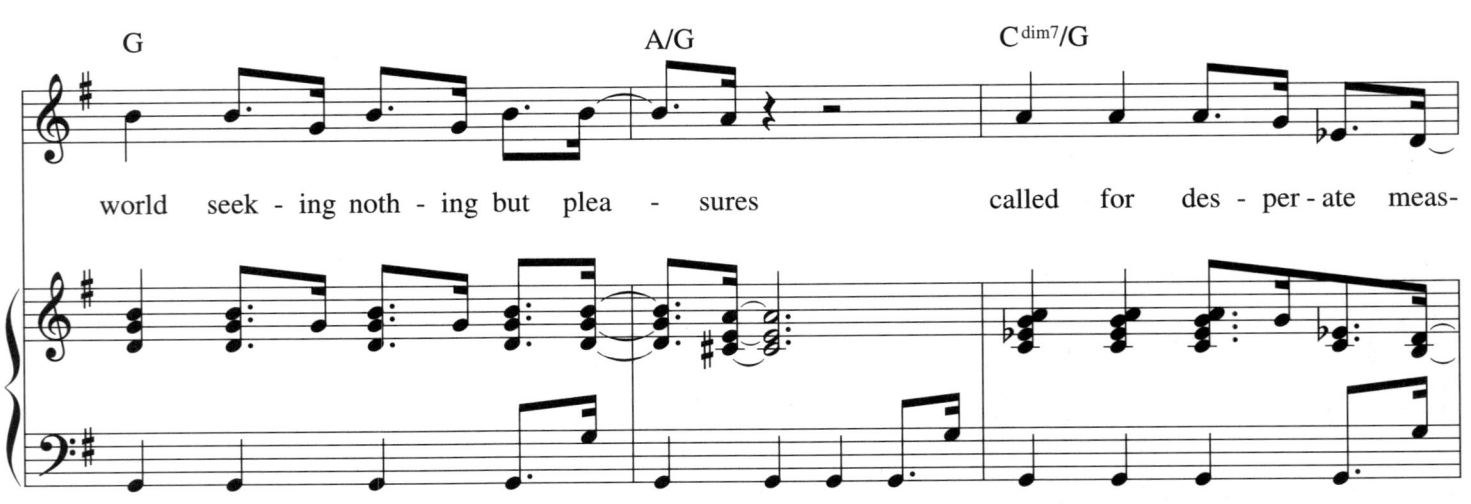

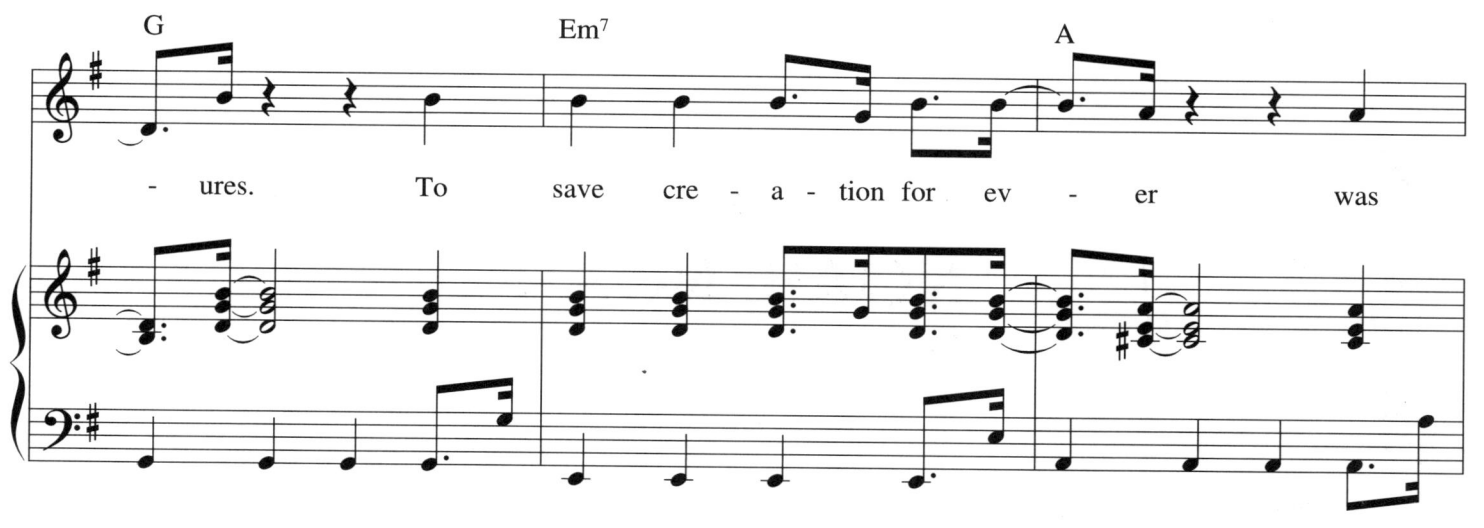
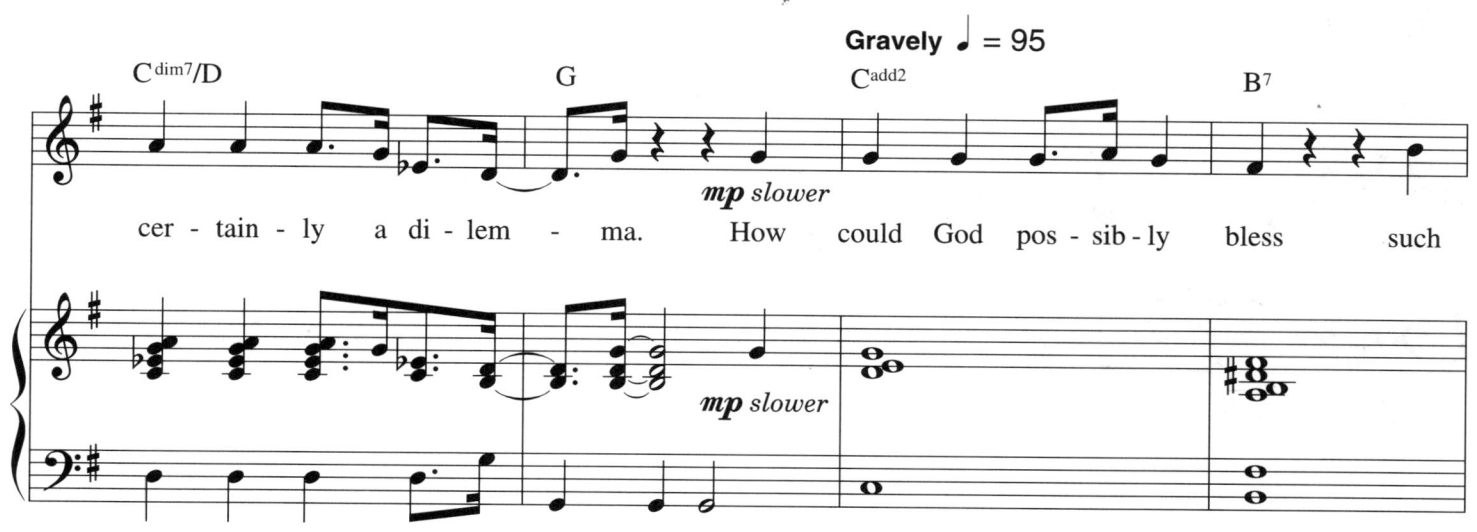

2
NOAH, NOAH
All + some two-part singing

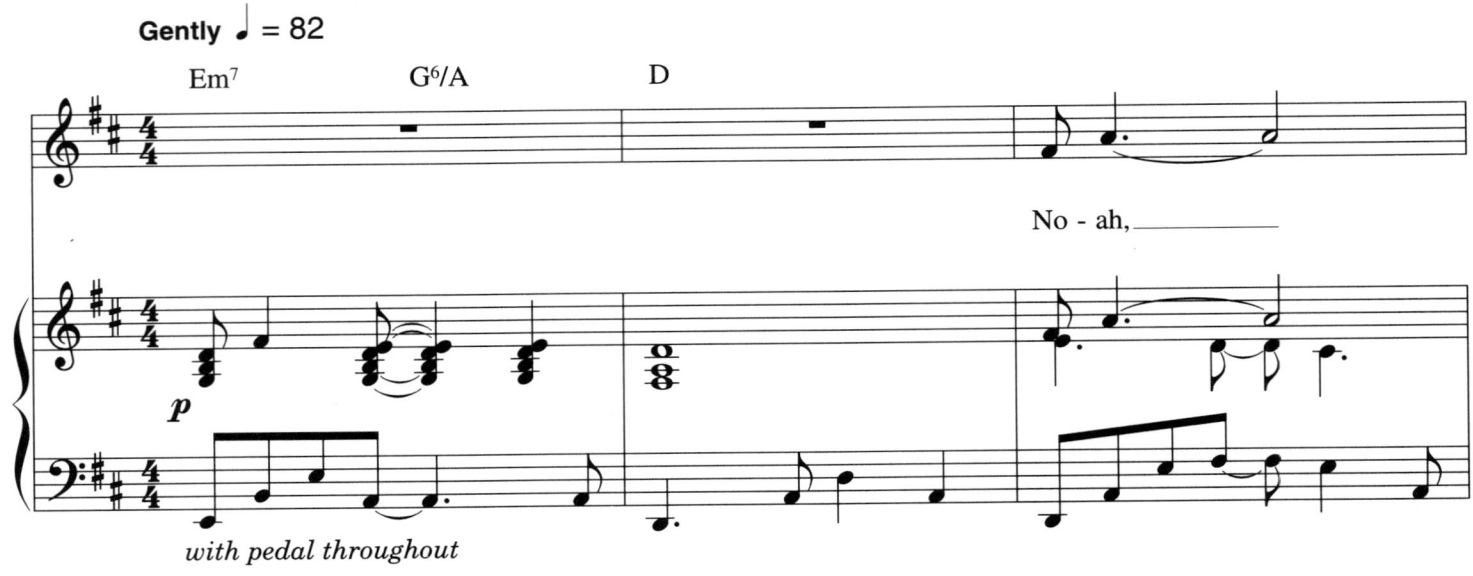

No - ah,

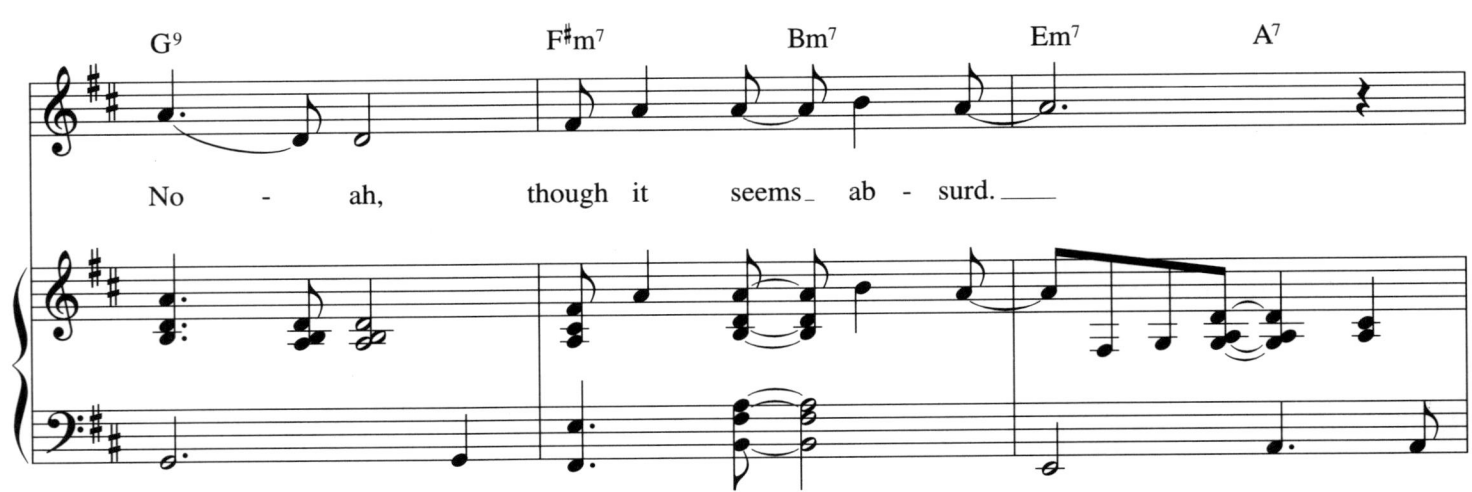

No - ah, though it seems ab - surd.

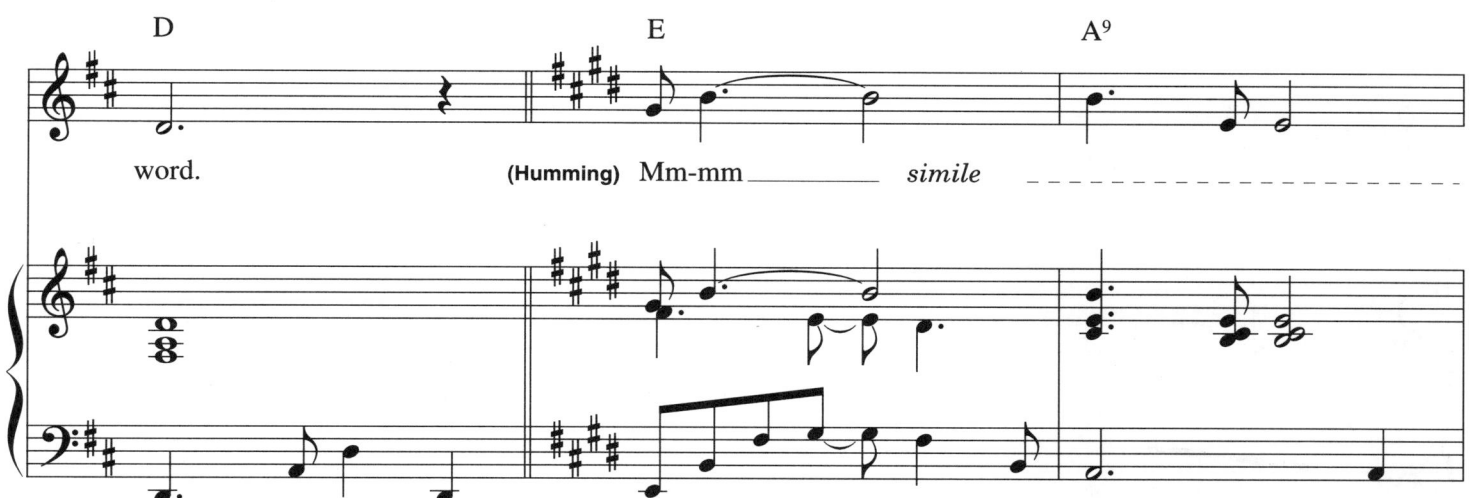

Note: The humming can be taken by a group or instrument if preferred.

7

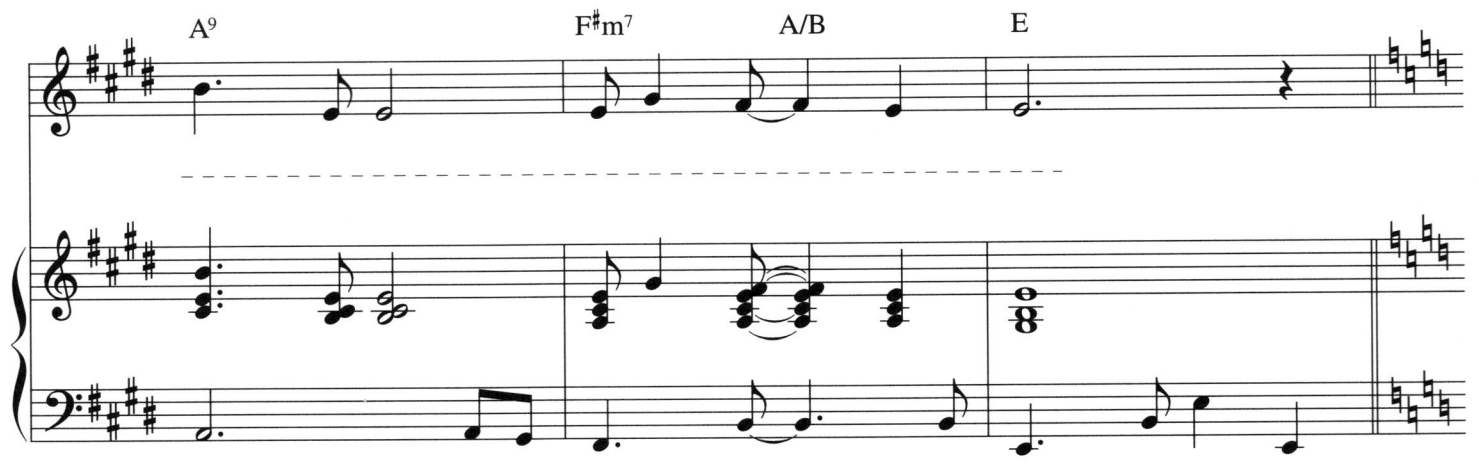

Narrator: "Noah was horrified when he heard the news, but, believing the word of the Lord, he started work at once on his boat." →

3
A LOAD OF BALONEY!
All

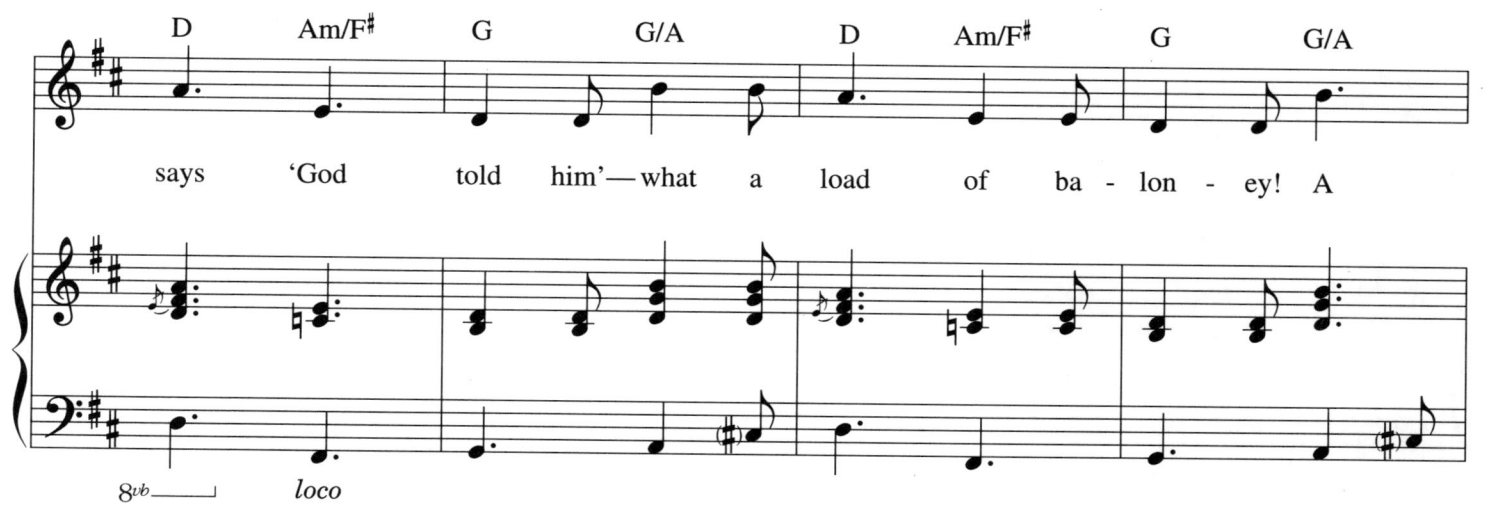

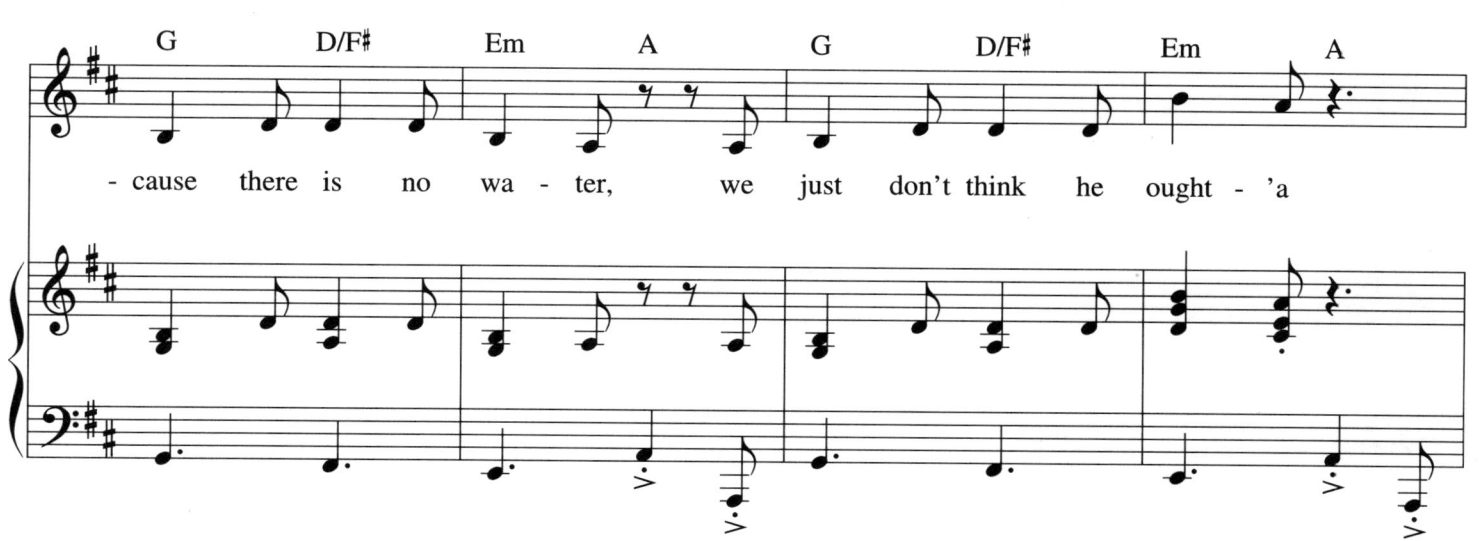

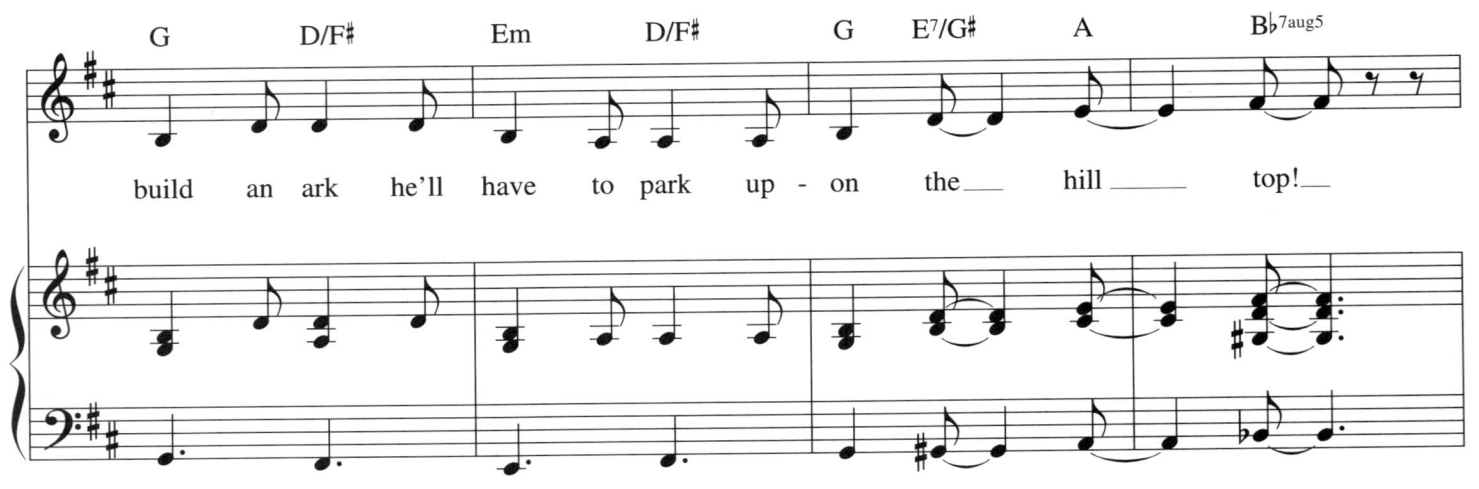
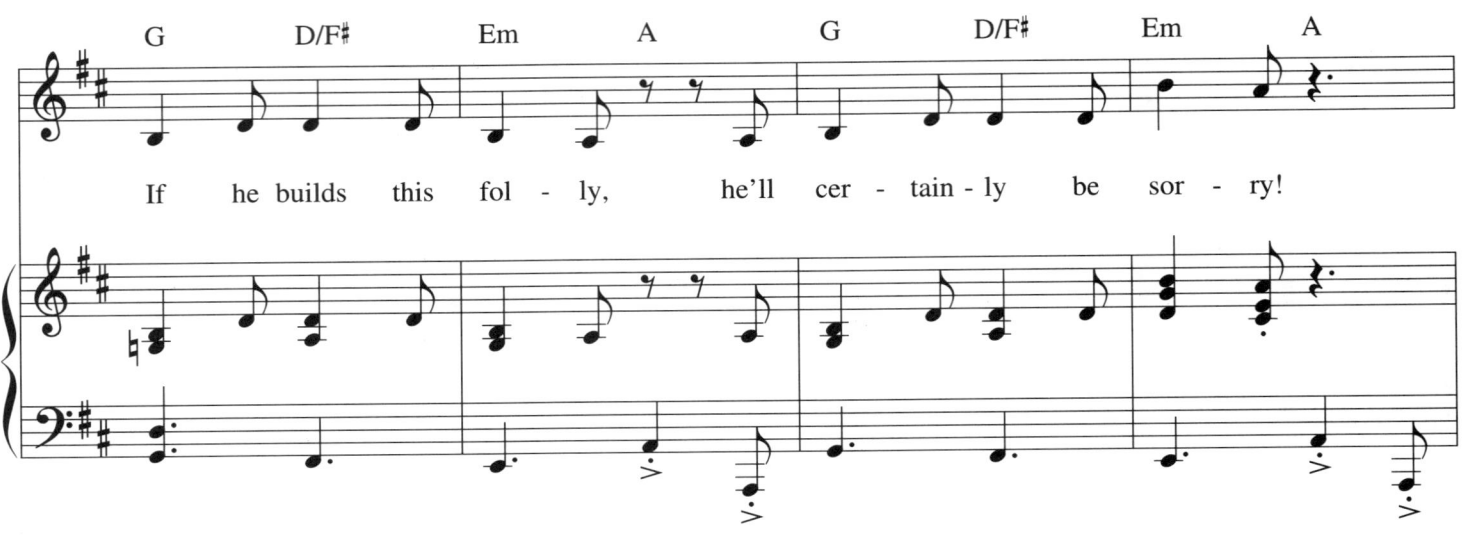

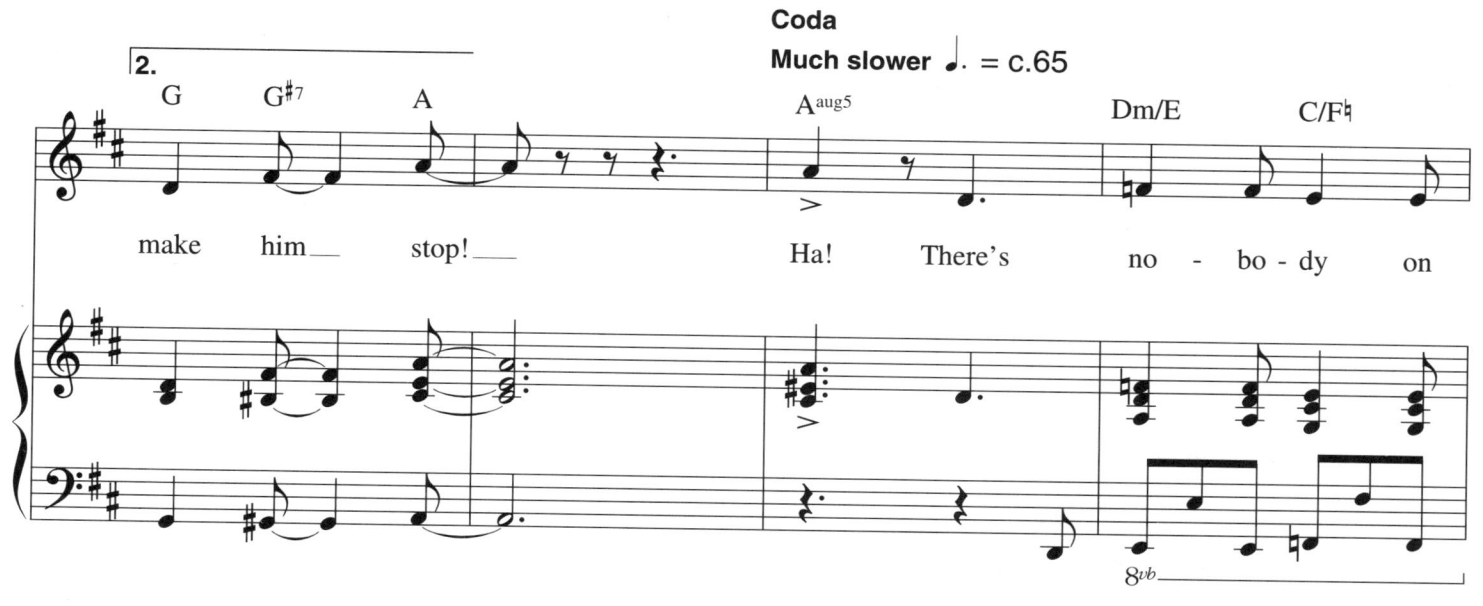

4A
MILES AND MILES AND MILES
All (could use groups for some verses)

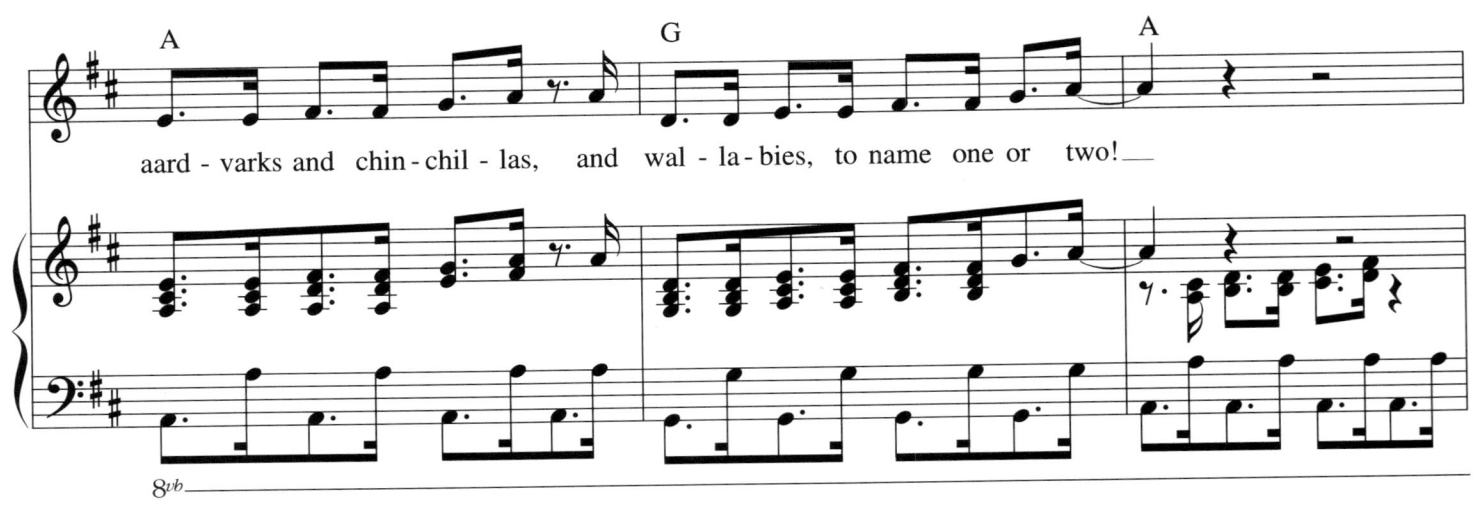

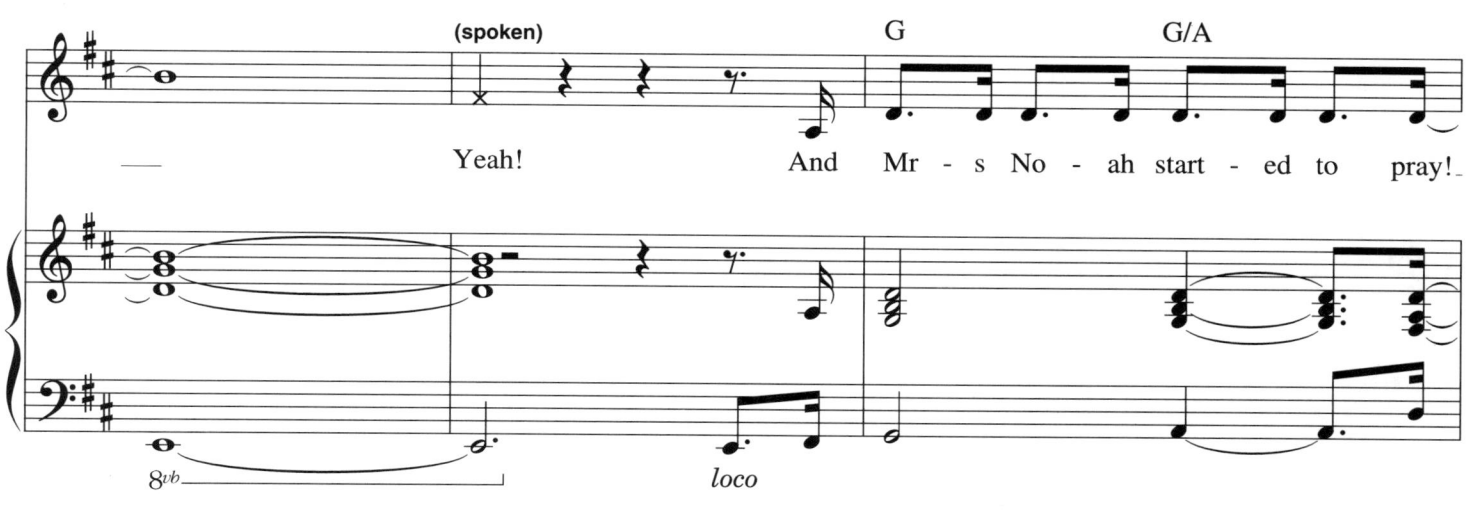

5A
ROCK THE BOAT
Noah solo

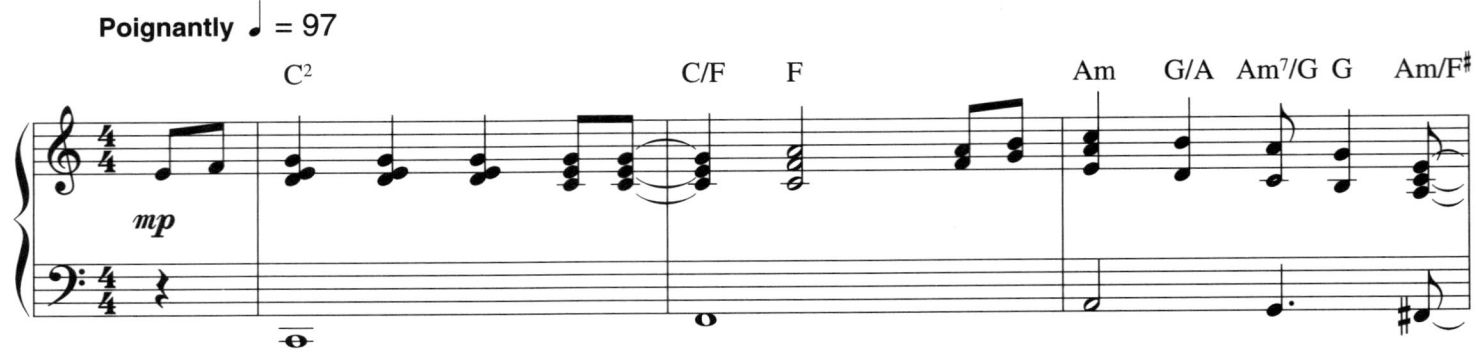

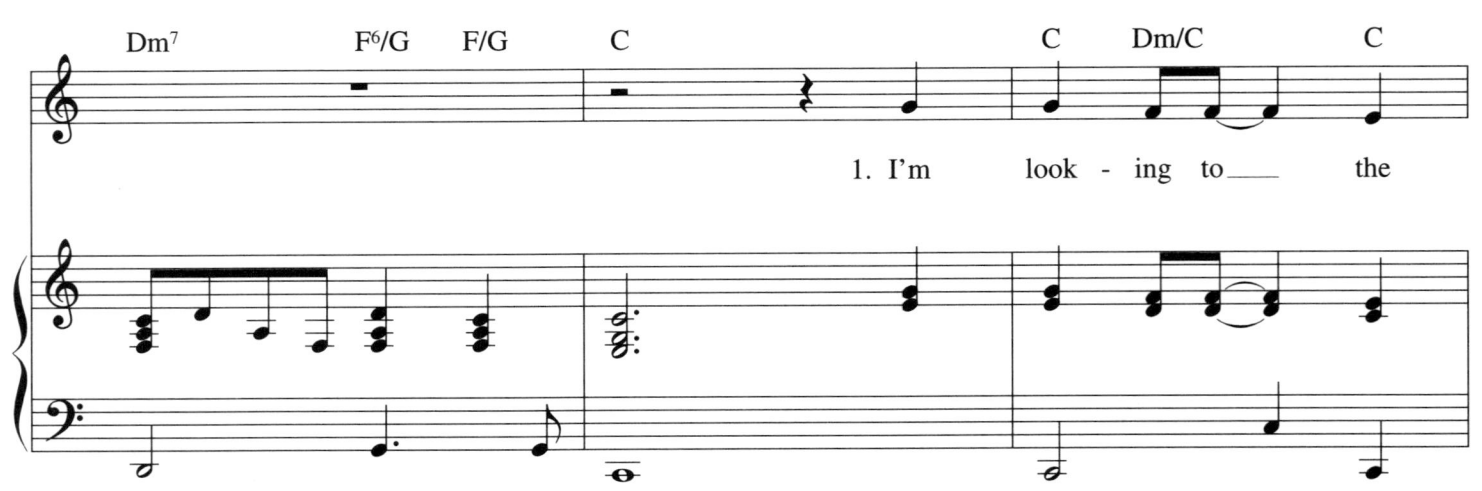

1. I'm look-ing to___ the

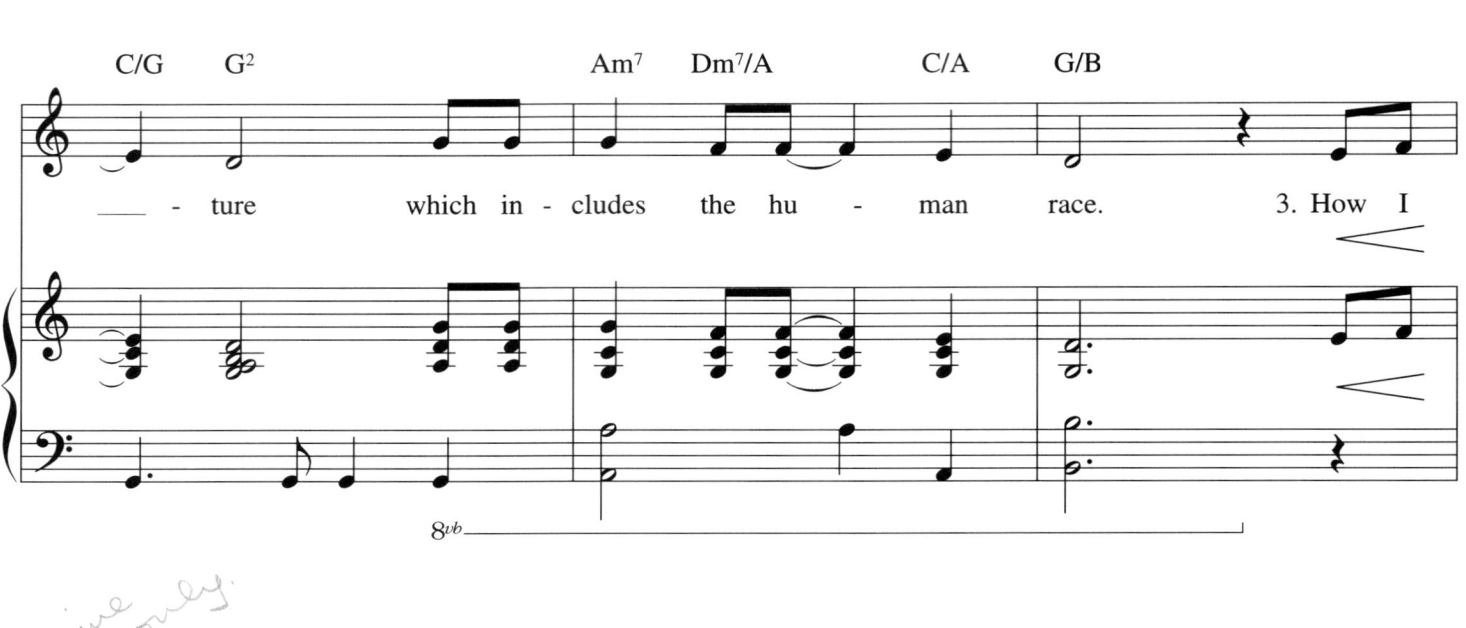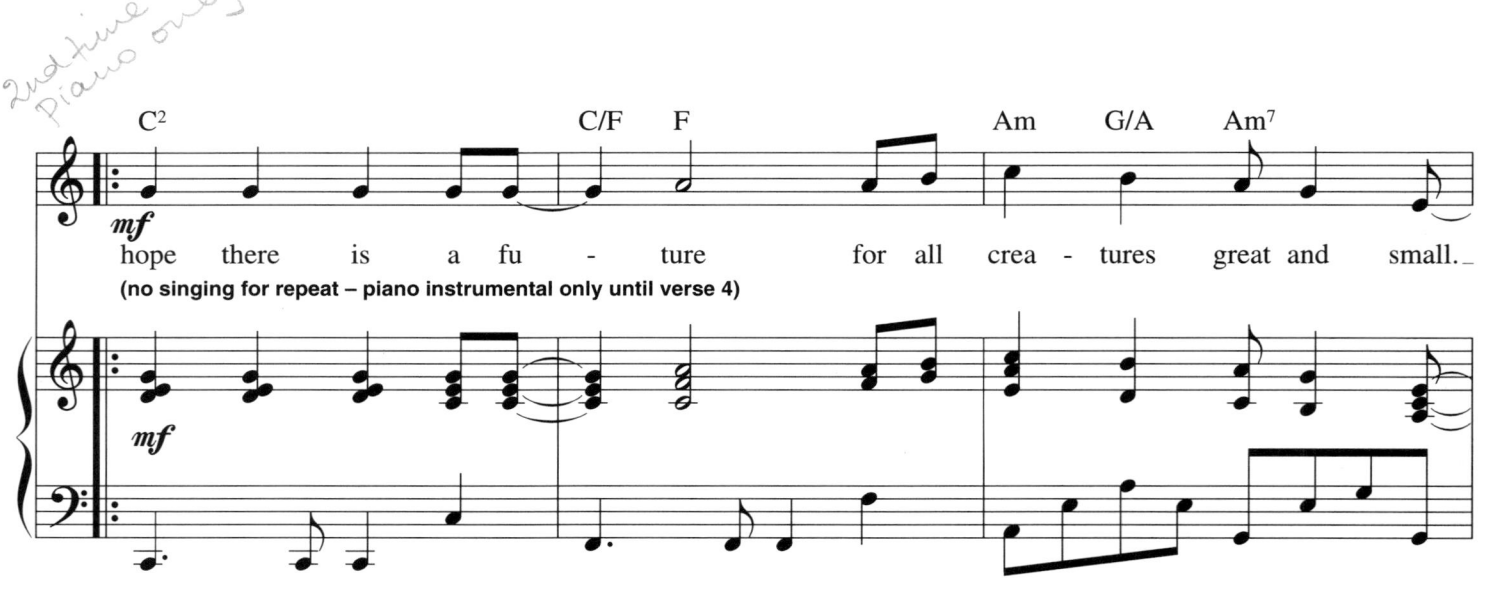

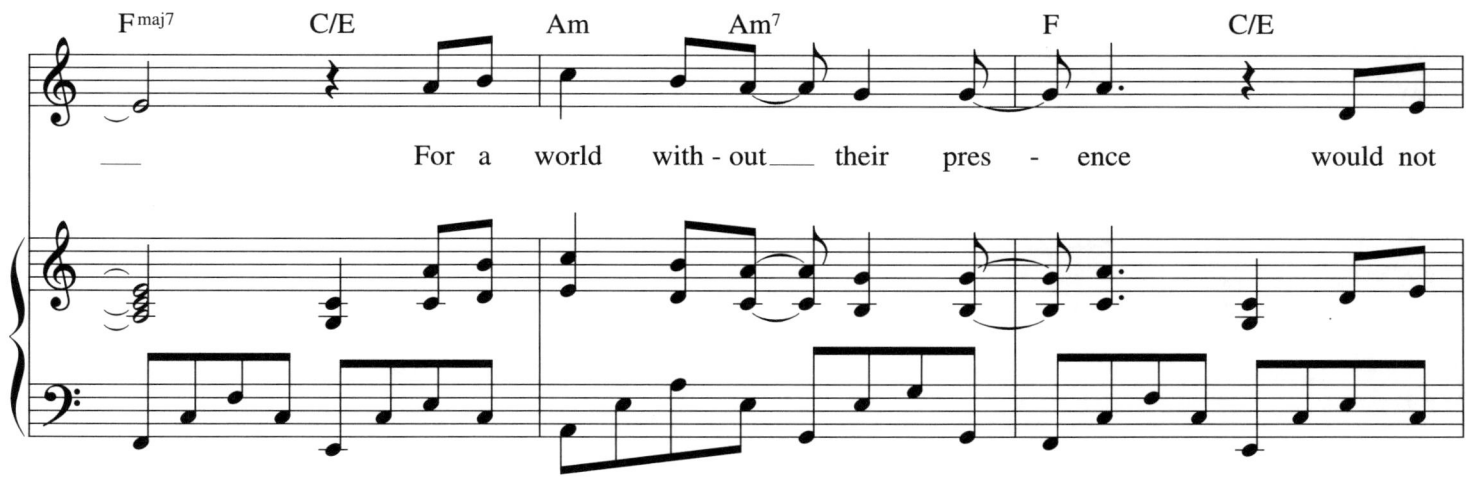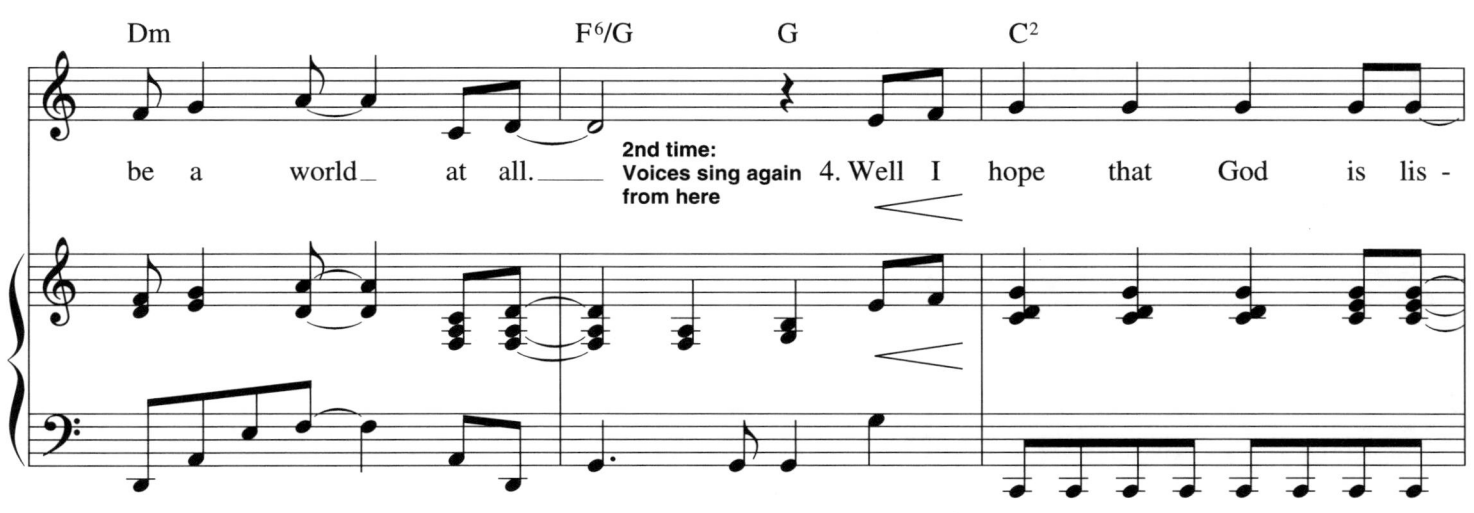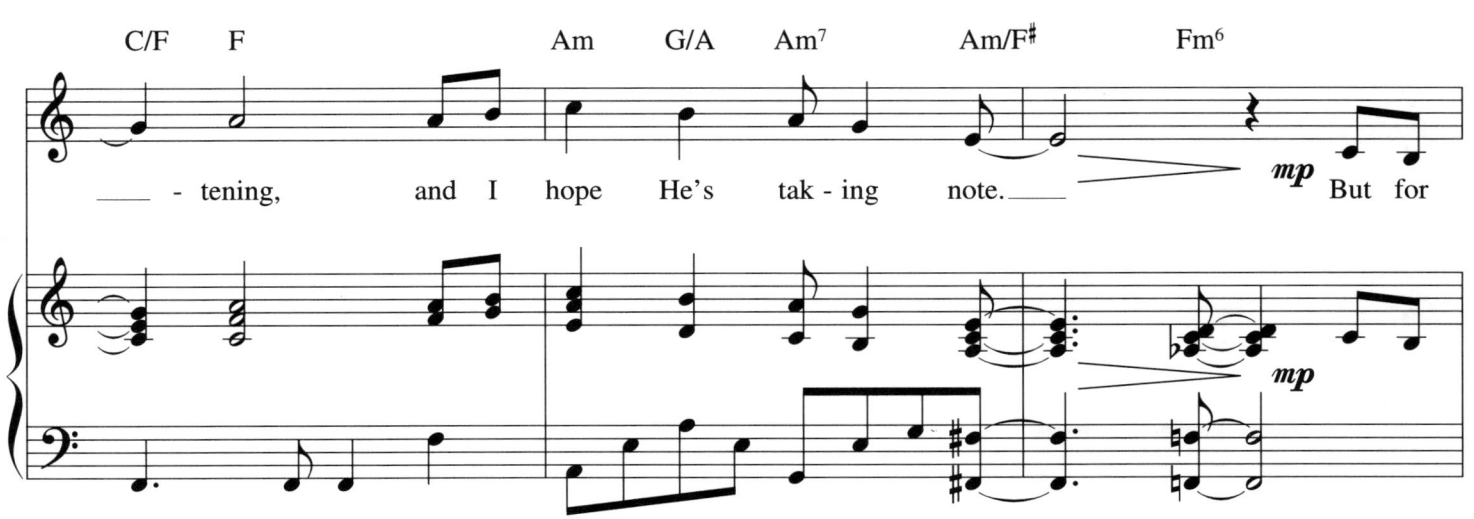

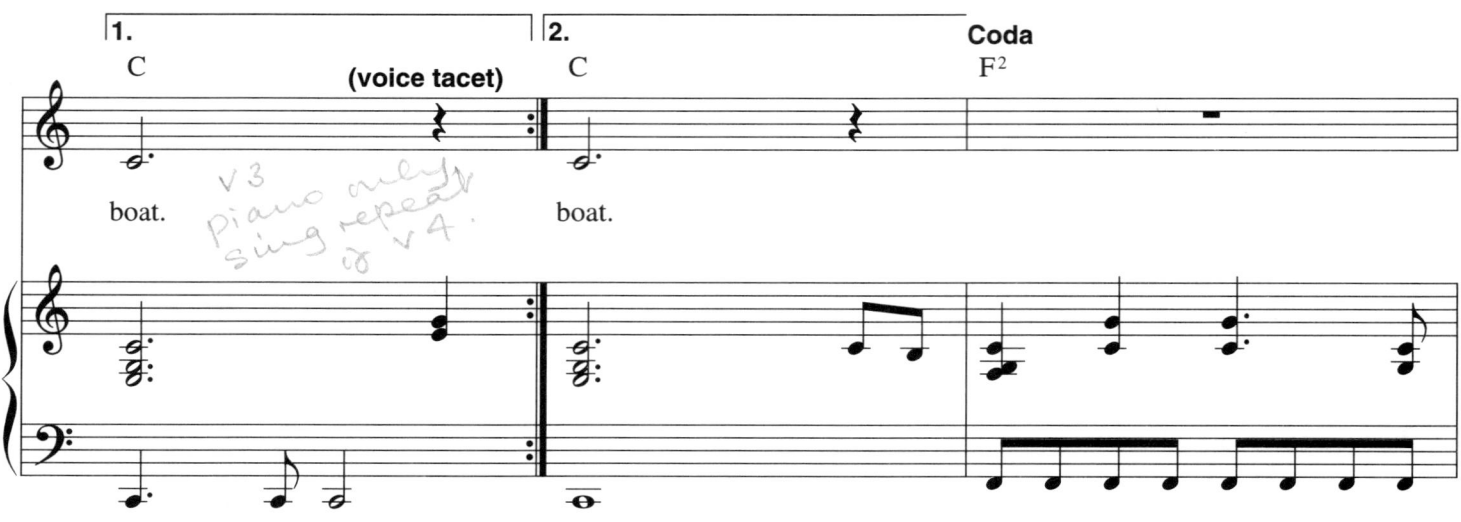

4B
A BIT OF A DO!
All + 'thigh-slapping' interlude

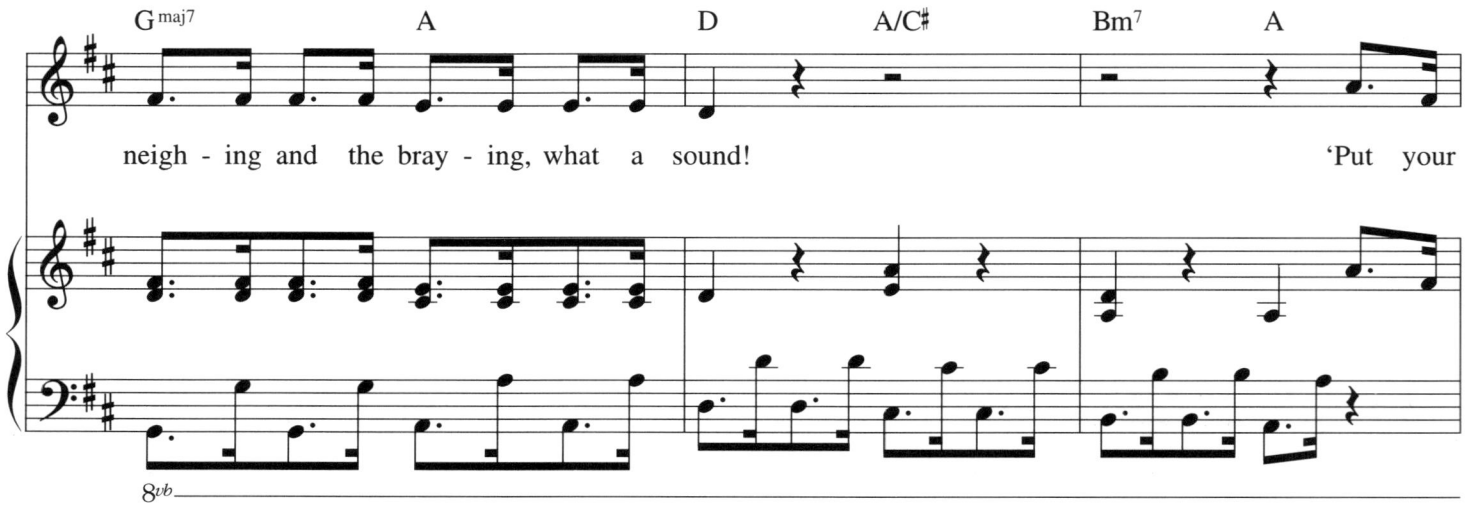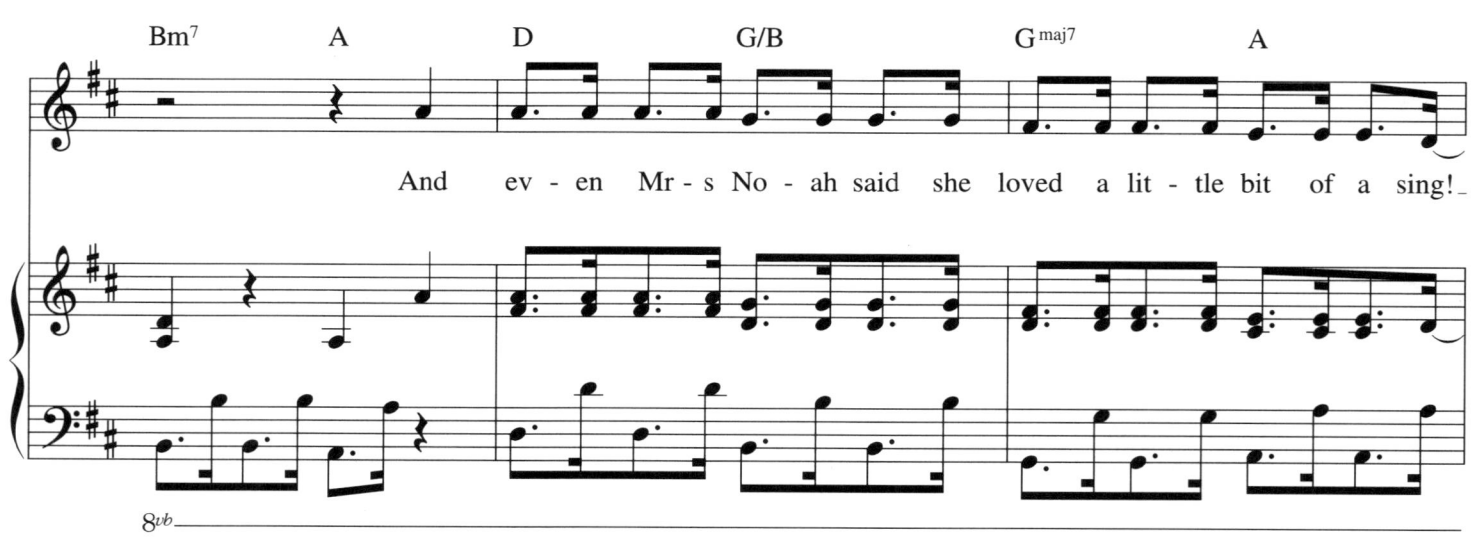

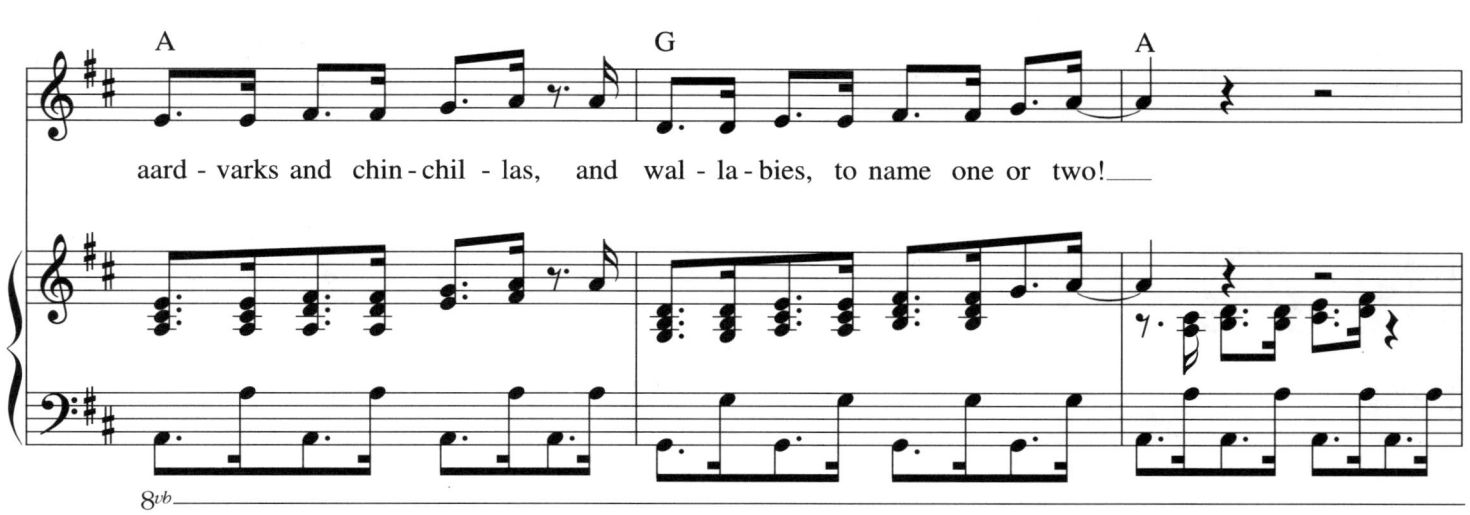

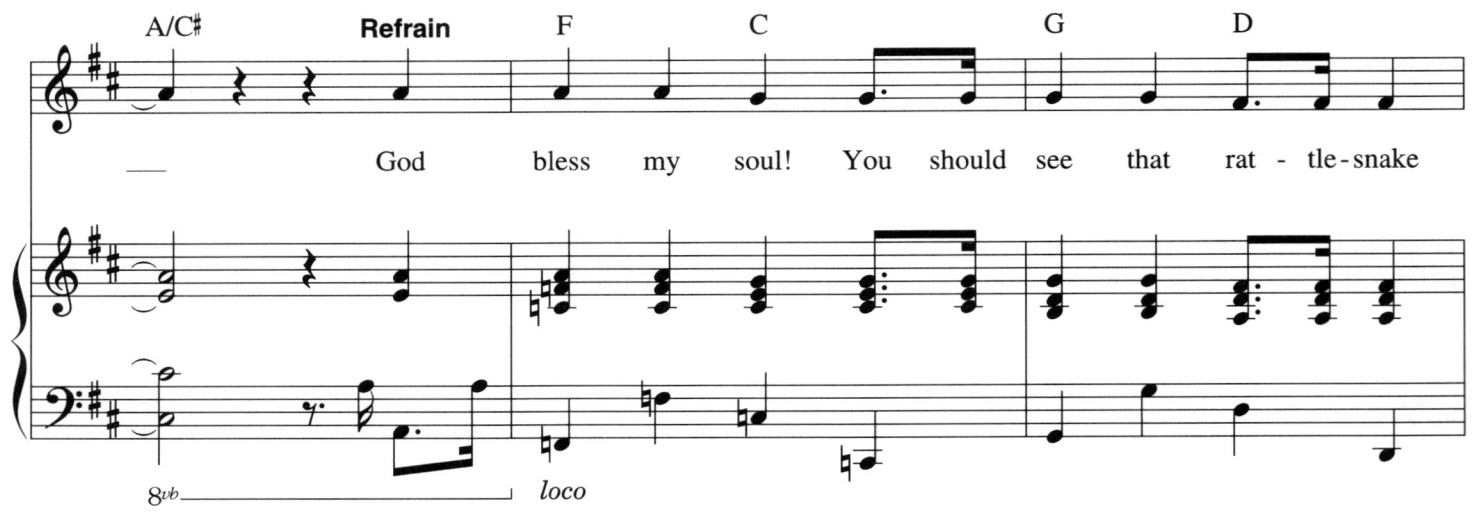
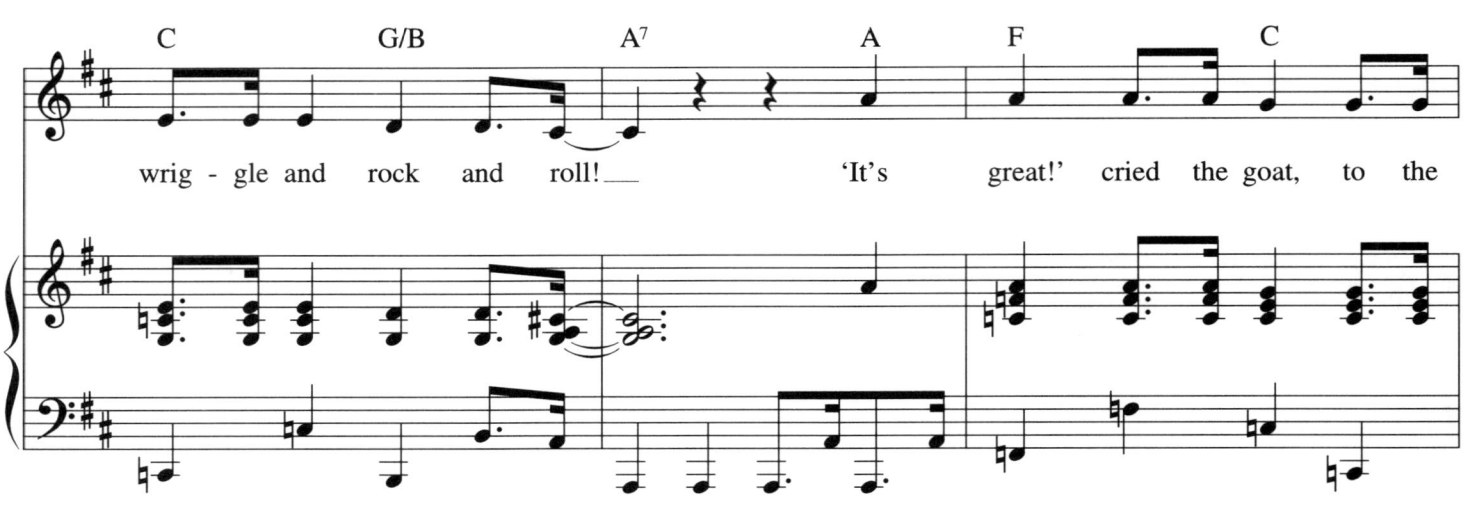

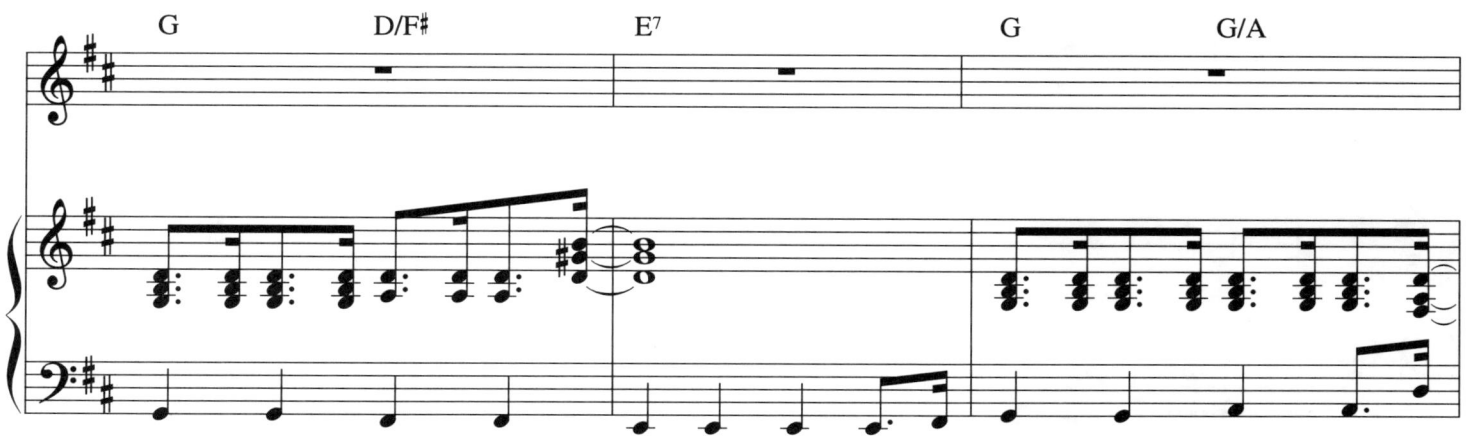

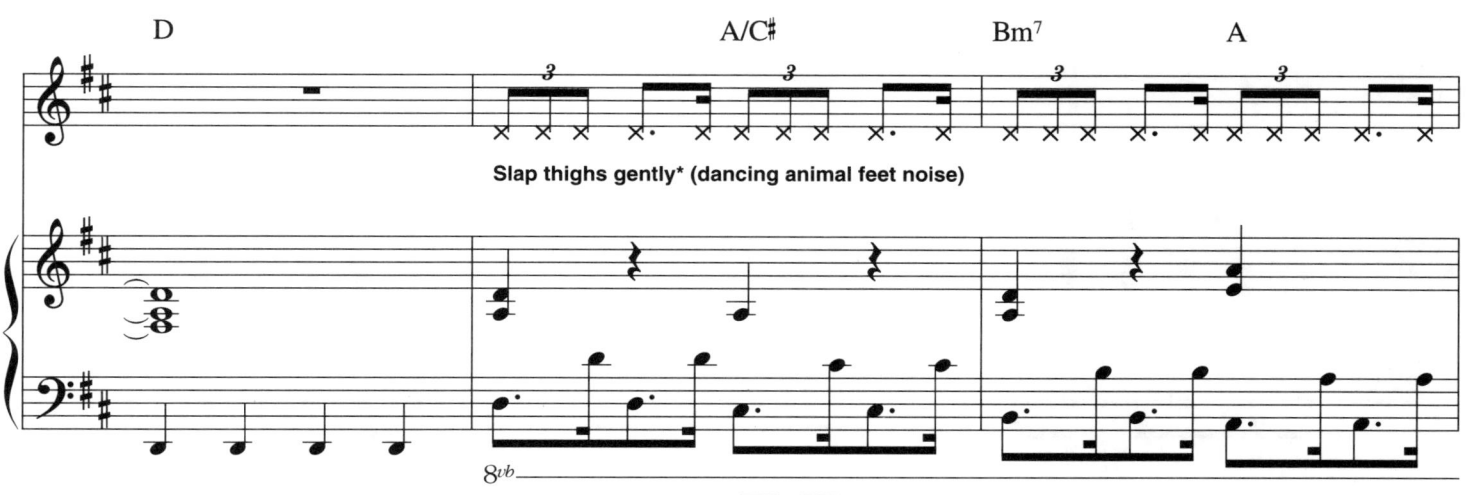

* If this is too hard, do [rhythm] throughout.
To add to the fun, you may wish to add "animal noises" every 1 or 2 bars!
Suggested examples: tigers, monkeys, dogs, parakeets, hyenas,
pigs, horses, gorillas, donkeys, owls, elephants . . .

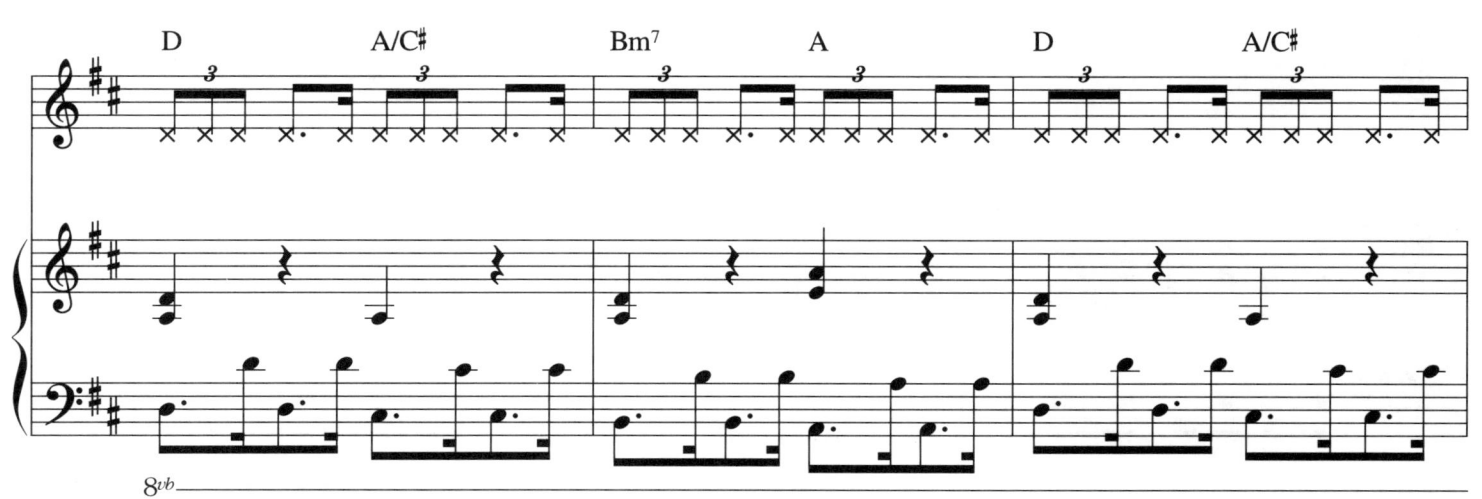

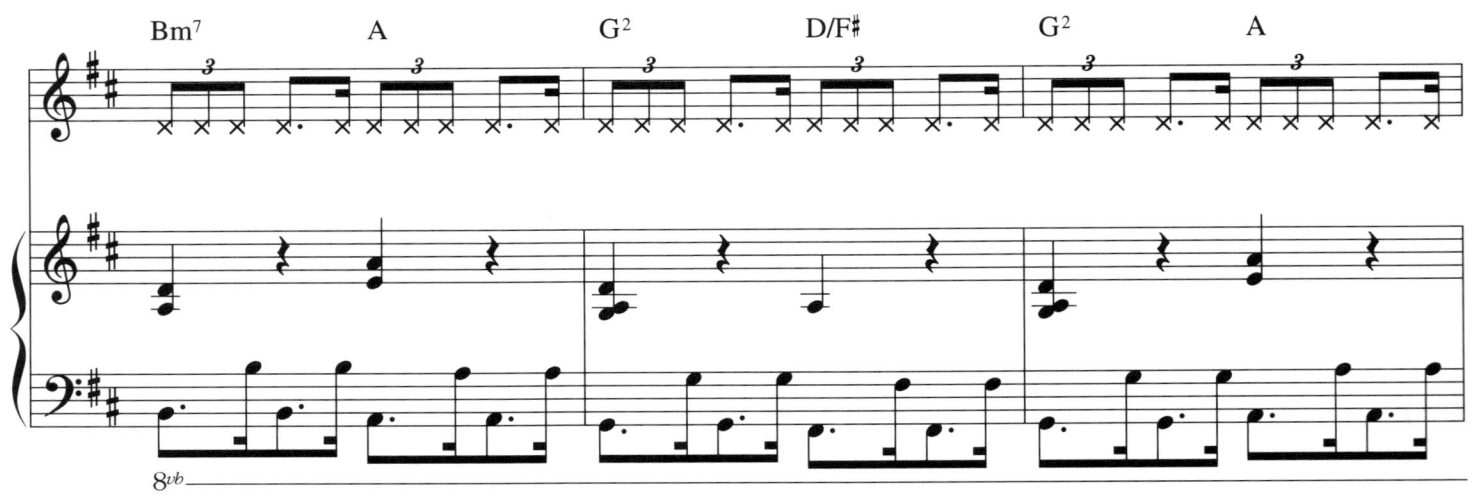

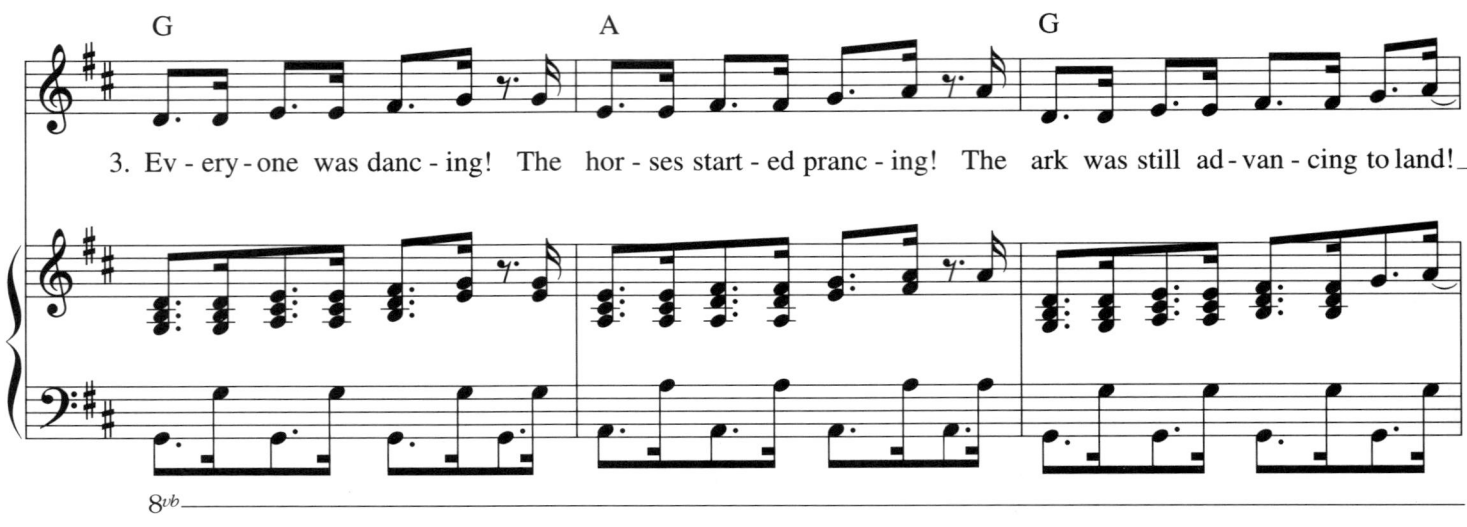

3. Ev-ery-one was danc-ing! The hor-ses start-ed pranc-ing! The ark was still ad-van-cing to land!

A nice con-strict-ing bo-a cud-dled Mrs No-ah, while

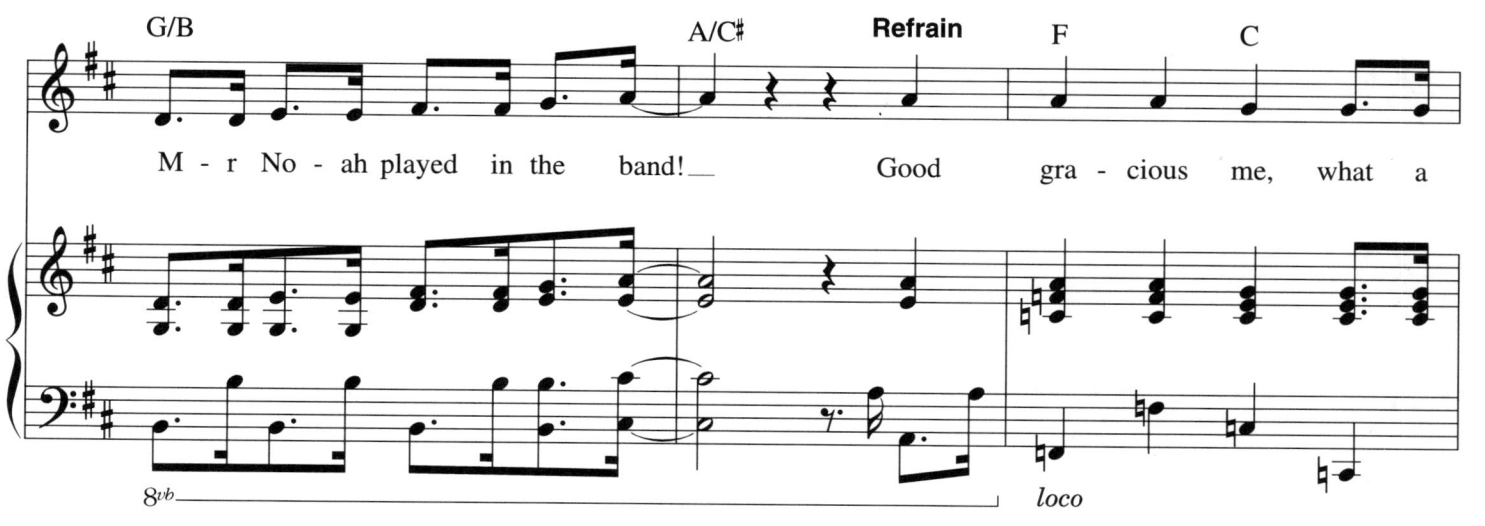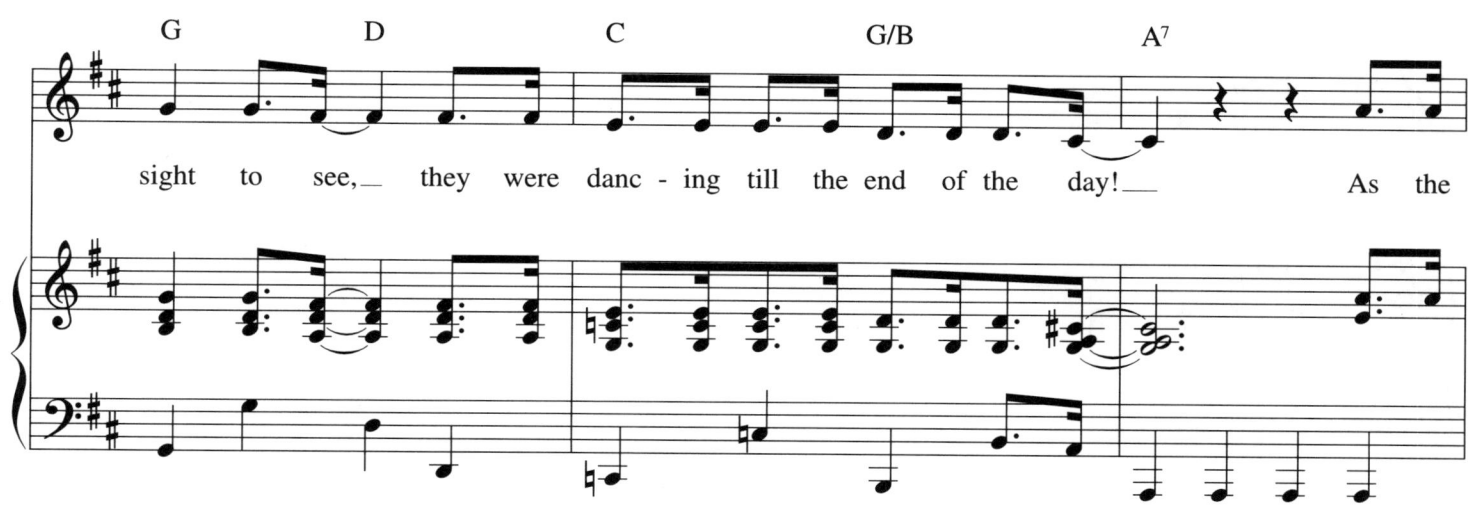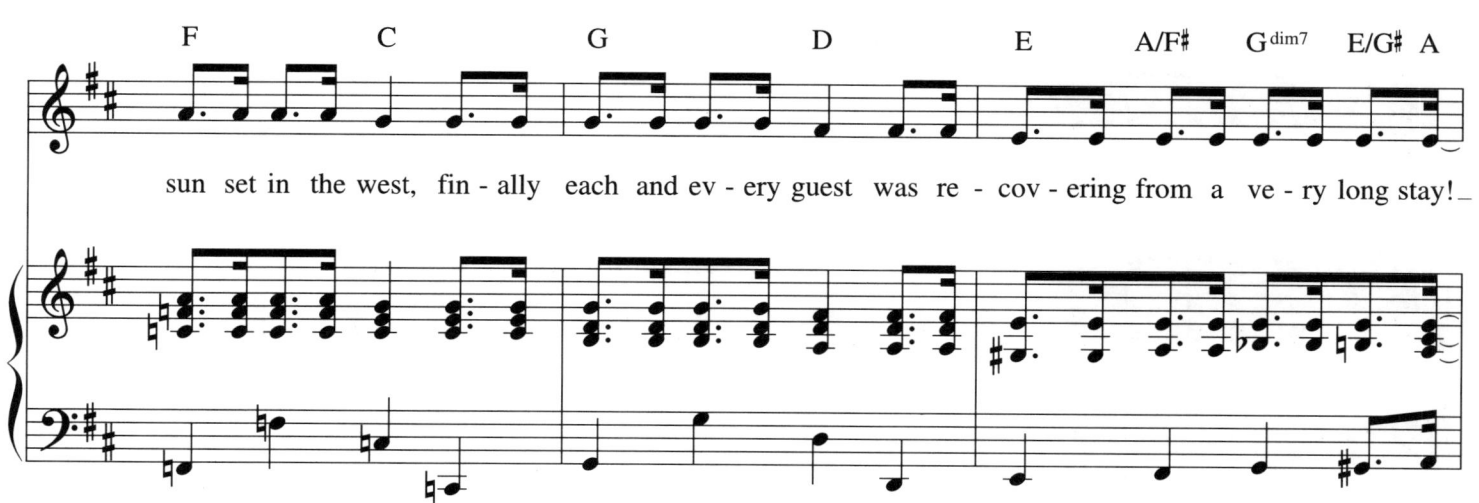

Enter Dove/Raven

35

5B
LIVE IN PEACE
All

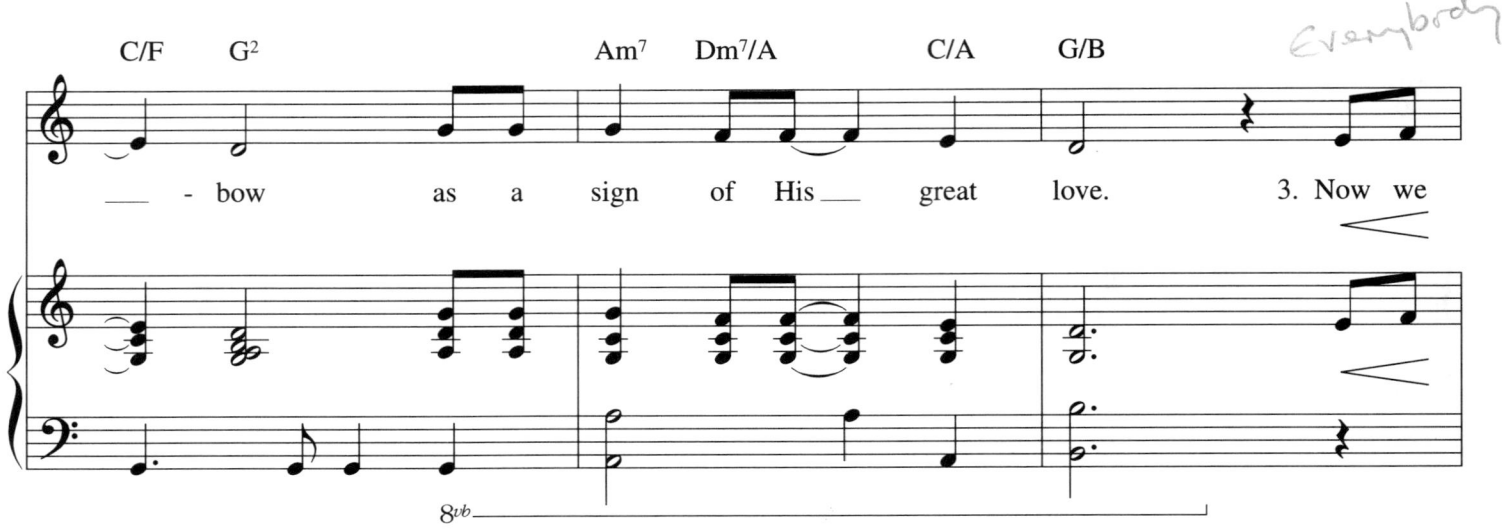
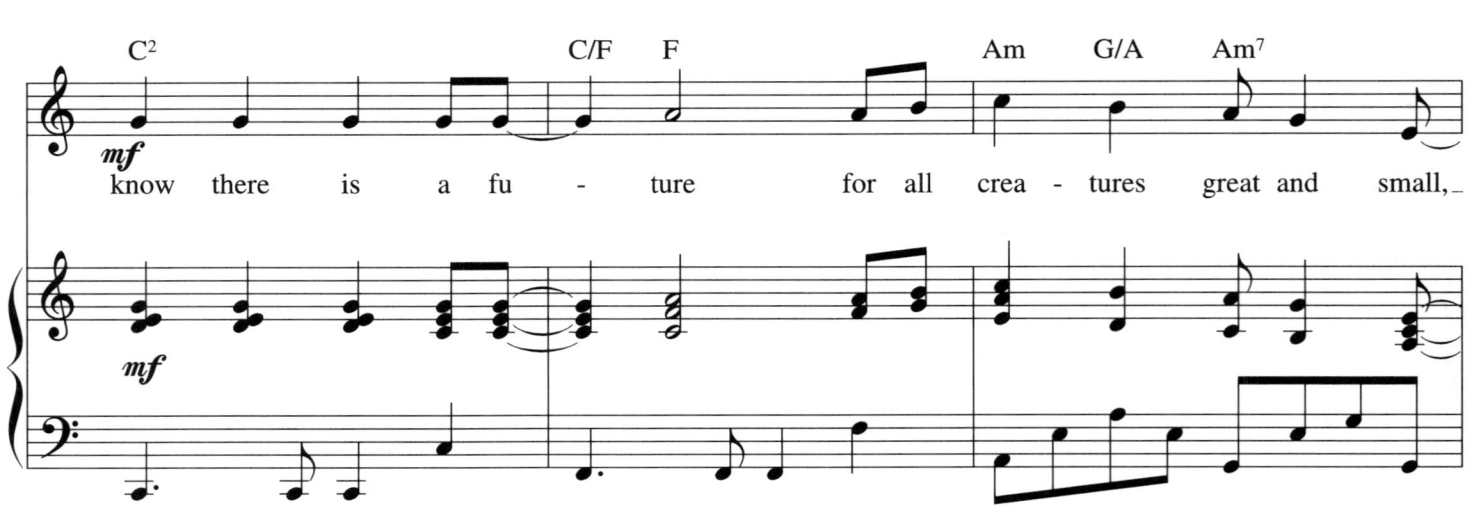

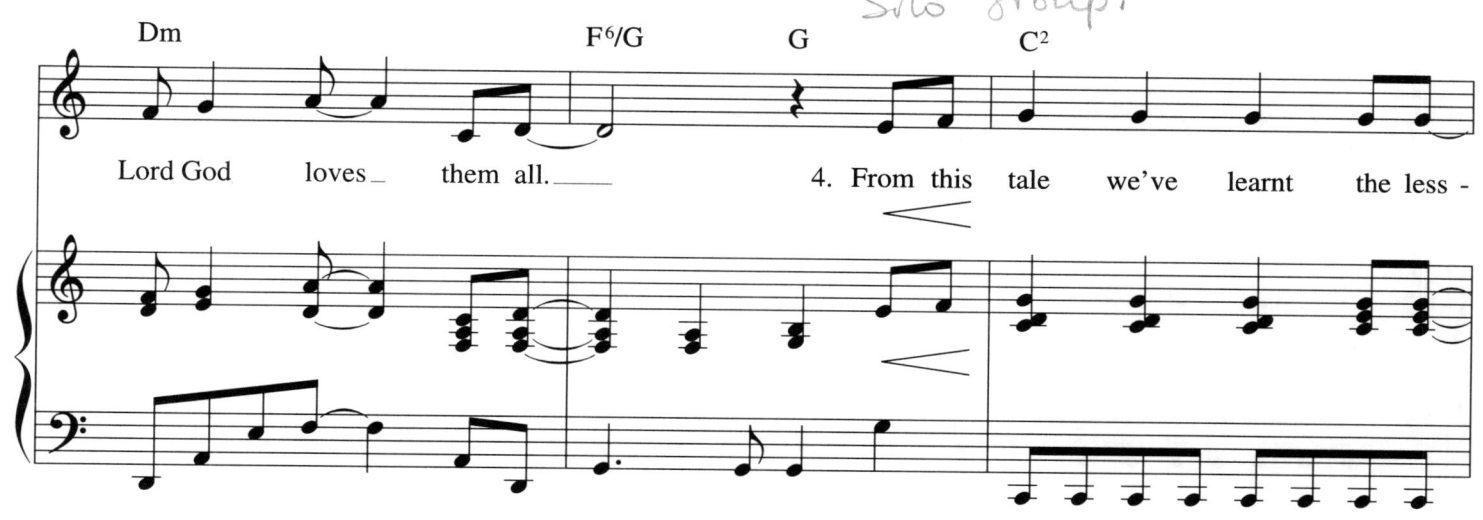

Author's footnote

"I wrote this musical in response to several requests and I have enjoyed myself enormously in the process. The more I thought about Noah, the more impressed and inspired I've been by him, and I hope you will be as well. I also hope Mrs Noah will forgive me for making her the subject of some light-hearted humour. I actually think highly of her too, but after this she may not think much of me!"

Sheila Wilson

Printed in Great Britain by Printwise (Haverhill) Limited, Haverhill, Suffolk 28430 (8/97)